The Ve

YOUR GUIDE TO KETOGENIC LOW CARB DIET WITH HIGH FAT AND PROTEIN RECIPES

Patrick Price

TABLE OF CONTENTS

INTRODUCTION 1

SECTION I: 2

    CHAPTER 1: INTRODUCTION TO VEGAN AND KETOGENIC 2

        Introduction to veganism 2

        Introduction to ketogenic diet 3

    CHAPTER 2: VEGAN-KETOGENIC DIET: COMBING THE TWO 5

    CHAPTER 3: HISTORY OF VEGAN KETOGENIC DIET 7

SECTION II 8

    CHAPTER 4: BASIC PRINCIPLES OF VEGAN KETOGENIC DIET 8

    CHAPTER 5: VEGAN KETO SHOPPING LIST 10

        Bad Carbs that Should be Removed from your Pantry 11

        Sources of Vegan Fats 12

        Sources of Vegan Proteins 13

        Baking 13

        Vegetables and Fruits 13

        Nut and Seeds 14

SECTION III: PLAN YOUR DIET 16

    CHAPTER 6: 7 DAYS VEGAN KETO DIET PLAN 16

        Monday 16

        Tuesday 17

        Wednesday 17

        Thursday 18

        Friday 18

Saturday 18

Sunday 19

List of Snacks and Desserts 19

CHAPTER 7: CHANGES TAKING PLACE IN BODY COMPOSITION 21

Avoid the sugar crashes 21

Flu-Like Symptoms 22

Can cause dizziness and fatigue 22

Might suffer from leg cramps 22

Reduced Physical Performance 22

SECTION IV: 24

CHAPTER 8: RECIPIES 24

Soy mush 24

Protein-power starter 26

Veggie Chili 27

Chopped Thai Salad with Coconut Curry Dressing 29

Scrambled Tofu 31

The Protein Vegan Salad 33

Asian Fusion Salad 35

Green Salad 37

SECTION V 39

CHAPTER 9: CONCLUSION 39

INTRODUCTION

You are a vegan and you are struggling to lose weight? You are desperate of how your body is looking at the moment?

This book is your solution! Congratulation, with acquiring this book, your journey of losing weight as a vegan begins today!

In this book, you will learn how to combine the ketogenic diet, which has helped millions of people losing their pounds and our vegan way of eating.

SECTION I:

CHAPTER 1:

INTRODUCTION TO VEGAN AND KETOGENIC

Introduction to veganism

Of course, as a vegan you know what is allowed to eat and what isn't, but for people who are unaware of the vegan diet, let me give a succinct introduction. A vegan diet is one that does not include meat. But not only that, it completely doesn't include any form of dairy products, like for example eggs or milk-products.

Despite all the allegations that Veganism is not a healthy form of life, the diet has proven to be a healthy one over the years.

A vegan diet includes almost every color in the rainbow, it includes fruits, vegetables, legumes, beans, and grains. The list can go on as there are infinite numbers of foods that can be made by combining the above food products. Also, since the diet has been around for almost 70 years now, it has become very common throughout the world. In our times, it is even possible to buy vegan versions of almost every food, such as ice creams, vegan mayonnaise, cheese and much more.

Introduction to ketogenic diet

Ketogenic Diet may have become popular in the last 15 years, but the concept is fairly old. It was first introduced around 1020 to a medical community. The diet was developed in order to help people suffering from epilepsy because the doctors realized that high-fat, low-carb diet was an effective way to stop seizures. Now, doctors have also realized that Keto diet is also helpful for many other neurological defects. One reason behind its effectiveness is that the ketones are really good when it comes to the brain.

People who are not suffering from any neurological diseases are also adopting this diet lifestyle as they have understood its effectiveness and usefulness. Ketogenic Diet commonly known as Keto is basically a combination of low-carb spread with a good mixture of healthy fats. One reason this diet has become famous is that it is really good for losing weight at the same time, the diet also increases brain power.

Meaning of the word "KETOGENIC"

While you consume food, your body breaks down all the carbohydrates present in the food into glucose. This glucose is what acts as a fuel for your everyday functioning. The idea behind the ketogenic diet is to reduce the number of carbohydrates and force the body to enter the Ketosis state. It is a state in which the body burns its fat instead of the carbs that you take in. The process starts when your liver releases ketones. You can call ketones as a flip switch between utilizing fat reserves and burning glucose.

The important thing to remember is that if you are not following the Ketogenic diet to perfection, it will lead to a number of medical situations. For instance, your body can produce too many ketones in uncontrolled diabetes and this can make you sick. Therefore, whenever you are following a Ketogenic diet, it is imperative that you follow it correctly.

CHAPTER 2:

VEGAN-KETOGENIC DIET: COMBING THE TWO

In the above chapter, we have explained both Vegan and Ketogenic diet individually. Nonetheless, the focus of this chapter is going to be on a form of diet that came into existence by combining these two i.e. Vegan and Ketogenic. It is called the Vegan Ketogenic Diet.

Ketogenic diet lately has become the ultimate diet in terms of fat loss and ethical consumption, but meeting in the middles is never without any compromise. The traditional Ketogenic diet is mainly based on consuming heavy animal fats, It would seem that Ketogenic diet and Vegan diet are two opposite sides of a coin. Reason being, the Ketogenic diet is structured based on a high fat to carb macronutrient ratio, whereas a Vegan diet requires a high carb to fat macronutrient ratio. So, depending on the side you are on, we are sure that you would have ample to support your cause. But the question here is, could these diets actually overlap? It is possible that you abide the principles of Veganism while you could enjoy the fat burning benefits of ketosis. The answer is Yes! You can enjoy the best of both diets while abiding the ethical principles.

According to the conventional Keto rules, a person is allowed only to consume 20g of net carbs every day. However, for a vegan Ketoers consuming 30g of net carbs is closer to achievable as compared to the original 20g especially when no meat is involved. Since all plant foods tend to have carbohydrates lieu of animals food that is low in carbohydrates. So, consuming plant foods is going to increase the number of carbohydrates.

If you want to maintain the 20g carbs routine, we can assure you that all you would be eating or we should say pouring would be oil in your mouth all day. Despite being boring, this is also very unhealthy. We already said, to come in the middle there has to be a compromise. So, you need to let go of the 20g carbs rule and increasing a little bit of the target number of carbs can really make your food tasty and delicious. However, to maintain ketosis, it is recommended to not go over 30g, there are many Vegan-Keto people who tend to consume up to 50g of carbohydrates and they still are losing weight while maintaining a healthy, cruelty-free lifestyle. It is very dependent on the individual.

Below is the correct macronutrients ratio required for Keto diet

- *5-10 percent of calorie should come from carbs, i.e. you can consume up to 20 grams of carbohydrates every day.*
- *15-30 percent of calories should come from protein*
- *60-75 percent of calories should come from fatty foods.*

CHAPTER 3:

HISTORY OF VEGAN KETOGENIC DIET

Vegan diet has been around for many decades; likewise, ketogenic has been around since the mid-90s'. However, Vegan Ketogenic diet is a fairly new concept. The idea became popular few years back when people understood that Keto is not only helpful for people suffering from mental disorders, but also for losing weight and maintaining a healthy lifestyle. But since a large number of people do not consume meat, which is a major part of the Keto diet, therefore, they came up with Vegan Ketogenic diet. This diet majorly composes of plant-based food. No animal products are incorporated into the diet and it seems the diet has become very effective and proven to be useful for many.

SECTION II

CHAPTER 4:

BASIC PRINCIPLES OF VEGAN KETOGENIC DIET

Like every other diet, there are also some basic principles of Vegan Ketogenic diet. These principles are imperative for you to follow in order to make the diet effective.

1. For starters, we understand that the counting process is integral, but counting is not really important, especially when you are starting out. You would need time to get a hand of things so a little cheating at the beginning isn't going to hurt. Make sure that you eat a good variety of foods and this is a satisfying and sustainable way of eating for you. Most of the people when starting the Keto diet, they tend to follow it very strictly, thus lose interest in very little time and eat up feeling miserable. This makes them quit before they could even see the output. So, for the first few days eat until you are content without keeping a close check on calories or carbs. However, this does not mean that you should not count at all. Just keep a watch but not that close.
2. Instead of the regular oils, you should use vegetable oils such as a good quality bottle of olive oil or a fine quality of coconut oil. The reason that we are emphasizing on a good quality oil is that a low-quality oil is bound to go rancid on store shelves and using these oils can cause more damage than they can help.
3. Since, you have made the decision to embrace Vegan Ketogenic diet, you need to make sure that you are

familiar with nuts. They are going to pay an important role in your diet plan. Rich with protein and fats, nuts are not only delicious, but they are also very filling. The best thing is that nuts are lower in carbohydrates as compared to many other plant-based foods.

4. Go green when on Vegan-Diet, as anything that is green tends to have very low carbs in it. These greens also become more bioavailable when cooked and consumed with fat. In other words, if you sauté the greens with olive oil and garlic, they not only become low carb food but also very tasty and easy to digest.

5. People are of under the belief that eating fruits in a Vegan-Keto diet is not allowed. We can explain how wrong they are. The main reason behind this assumption is the presence of sugar in the fruits. Although you can't consume every type of fruit, however, you can eat as many as berries you want. They are excellent as they are rich in nutrients and low in carbohydrates.

CHAPTER 5:

VEGAN KETO SHOPPING LIST

Once you have made up your mind that you want to join the league, the next step is to understand the difference between good carbs and bad carbs. You need to fill your pantry with Vegan-Keto food or in other words with good carbs, instead of the regular junk food or bad carbs. To get started, the first thing you need to do is SHOPPING. Something everyone loves!

When it comes to losing weight, the only thing that is important in a Keto diet is the number and type of carbs you consume every day. Nonetheless, to maintain your overall health and to attain your goal of losing weight, you (vegans) need to distinguish between bad carbs and good carbs.

Foods that are high in nutrients and fiber are said to be good carbs. On the contrary, all the heavily processed foods that are high in carbs are considered to be bad carbs. Reason being, these carbs enter the bloodstream faster as compared to good carbs because they are converted to sugar at a faster rate.

An effective Keto diet program requires a good source of protein, fat and some vegetables that should be easily available in your fridge. So, let's get started

Bad Carbs that Should be Removed from your Pantry

Below, we have formed a list of all the bad carbs that should be removed from your pantry under all circumstances. It is important to get rid of these heavily processed, high carb foods. The foods include

- Crackers
- Tortillas
- Chips
- Fruit Juices
- Carrots, Corn, Sweet Potatoes, Yams and Potatoes
- Non-Diet Sodas
- Sugar added, low fiber cereals
- White Bread
- White Rice
- White Pasta

Sources of Vegan Fats

Avocados, peanut butter, almond butter and coconut are some really good food of Vegan. Besides these, there are many other Fat options for example

- *Sesame Oil*
- *Olive Oil*
- *Flax Seed oil*
- *Coconut Oil*
- *Cocoa Butter*
- *Canola Oil*
- *Almond Oil*
- *Almond Butter*

Sources of Vegan Proteins

Despite the popular belief, most Tofu is really low in carbs along with noble bean (Tempeh). Both of these are excellent protein sources, but they are extremely low in carbs. Another thing that is rich in protein and low in the carb is textured vegetable protein. Then we have protein powder, each and everything is very easily available online and in almost every supermarket stores.

Baking

Gluten-free Vegan baking is the best way of filling your stomach without consuming anything that is unethical or high on carbohydrates. They use coconut and almond flour instead of the regular flour, and yet all the things turn out to be pretty amazing. Other things for baking that you should incorporate in your shopping list include

- Guar Gum
- Psyllium Husk
- Flax Seed Meal
- Coconut Flour
- Almond Flour

Vegetables and Fruits

You can eat a wide variety of vegetables and fruits, below is the list of all the vegetables and foods that you can eat.

- Zucchini
- Spinach
- Spaghetti Squash
- Radish

- Peppers
- Parsley
- Mushrooms
- Lettuce
- Kale
- Green Beans
- Garlic
- Fennel
- Eggplant
- Green Soybeans/Edamame
- Cucumber
- Celery
- Cauliflower
- Cabbage
- Brussels Sprouts
- Broccoli
- Bok Choy
- Avocado
- Asparagus
- Artichokes

Nut and Seeds

They are an important part of your Vegan-Keto diet, so you need to incorporate a good amount of them in your diet.

- Walnut
- Sunflower Seeds
- Sesame Seeds
- Pumpkin Seeds
- Pecans

- Macadamias
- Hazelnuts
- Coconut Flakes
- Chai Seeds
- Cashews
- Almonds

SECTION III: PLAN YOUR DIET

CHAPTER 6:

7 DAYS VEGAN KETO DIET PLAN

Once everything that we believe to be bad carbohydrates are removed from our pantry, the next step is to work on a good diet plan for a week. Why week? For beginners, we suggest that they take it slow, after all "Slow and Steady Wins the Race". You people might be vegans, but you for sure are not used to the Keto dieting style. Therefore, it is imperative for you to first get a hang of it, before you fully devote yourself to it.

One think that we can promise you is that you won't get bored by the food options, as there are going to be a lot of them. Below, we have made a 7 days vegan Keto Diet plan.

Monday

The first day of a week and also the best time to start with your new diet plan. Excited? So are we, so let's get to work.

Breakfast: There is a long list of things that you can eat your breakfast, but ensure that you enjoy your breakfast. You can enjoy a taste Soy-mush in the morning.

These are generic categories, what type of fruit you eat, solely depends upon you. However, you do remember that on our shopping list, berries were the only fruits that we bought. So, you need to choose among those fruits that we stocked in our pantry.

Lunch: For lunch, you can enjoy any green salad, let's eat something chili. You can have a good amount of veggie chili.

Snack: For people like us, who feel hungry every other hour, the Vegan-Keto diet offers a variety of snacks. You can enjoy a handful of raw almonds along with some berries.

Dinner: Take a good size bowl of Vegetable salad and also, if you still feel hungry you can enjoy some more veggie chili.

Tuesday

Still excited? Good because today we will be having another exciting menu.

Breakfast: Take the soy-much again in the morning, it gives you a kick start-morning.

Lunch: Enjoy a bowl of the Scrambled Tofu.

Snack: Cucumber slices with Olive and Mushroom Tapenade

Dinner: Again, enjoy a good amount the Scrambled Tofu, for desert you can have some berries

Wednesday

A bright new day, with a brighter and look forward to menu

Breakfast: Have some really amazing Protein-power starter

Lunch: Enjoy a Good Vegetable Salad.

Snack: For snacks, you can enjoy Sun-dried Tomatoes and raw almonds

Dinner: We have sesame stuffed Portobello mushroom along with black beans and to spice things up, you can enjoy them with mixed vegetable salad.

Thursday

You have reached the mid-way, good going

Breakfast: Protein-power starter

Lunch: Veggie Chili

Snack: Mushrooms stuffed with Pine Nuts and Spinach

Dinner: Vegetable salad along with stuffed Eggplant

Friday

The last working day, but also a day to enjoy some really amazing food.

Breakfast: Soy-mush

Lunch: Chopped Thai Salad

Snack: Cucumber slices with Olive and Mushroom Tapenade

Dinner: Green vegetable salad.

Saturday

Breakfast: Enjoy some berries with nuts and soy yoghurt.

Lunch: Have the amazing Protein Vegan Salad

Snack: For snacks, you can enjoy Sun-dried Tomatoes and raw almonds with some berries as desert.

Dinner: Veggie Chili.

Sunday

Breakfast: Enjoy the tasty Ezekiel Cereal with berries and nuts

Lunch: Have a good serving of scrambled Tofu

Snack: Assorted Raw Vegetables served Spinach dip.

Dinner: Vegan Sloppy Joes, served with a Green Vegetable Salad.

Done, you have just finished a week, and we are sure that you have enjoyed every moment of it.

List of Snacks and Desserts

In-case you are have a good appetite and even after having a good portion of lunch or dinner, you still feel hungry, then you can always choose from one of these desserts of snacks to add to your diet. They will not only help you get rid of the hunger, but they are also very healthy and low in carbs.

- Still hungry, you can always throw in a bowl of any green salad you like.
- If salad is not a thing that you want to eat, you can have avocado but make sure that it is not more than half and to add more taste to it, you can have it with pink Himalayan salt.
- You can also enjoy an amazing cup of vegetable stock; the best is always home-made
- You can add Kombucha in your breakfast, but beware that they are pretty high on carbs. So, include rarely and very little amount.
- Enjoy a handful of roasted or raw nuts and seeds. In-case you want to eat more and want to enjoy more of the

health benefits, you should soak nights before having them.
- Fruits, by fruits we mean berries. You can eat frozen or fresh, whatever you like.
- Take a silicon ice tray and put a tablespoon of coconut oil in it. Place that into your fridge for overnight. Once it is settled, you can now enjoy a snack that looks like ice, if not taste like one.

CHAPTER 7:

CHANGES TAKING PLACE IN BODY COMPOSITION

It is but natural that your body's composition change when you change your eating habit. A slight change in your eating patterns causes your body to act and react differently, what to say about the change of your entire eating regime.

Vegan Ketogenic diet is a very different form of dieting as compared to the regular diet plans. A lot of time is required for your body in order to adjust with it, especially when you are a meat lover. We already know that in standard diets, the carbs that we intake are broken into glucose, the main source of energy for your body. The utilized glucose is stored in your muscles and liver in the form of glycogen for future use.

Meanwhile, the aim of Vegan Keto diet is to change this entire process. When you go on Keto diet, your body is bound to go into glycogen-deprived state due to the fact that you have cut down your intake of carbs. Fat is used in lieu of carbs to produce energy.

Avoid the sugar crashes

The energy that you get from fat burns is slower as compared to the bursts of energy that you obtain from the glucose. So, your body is bound to go crazy after some sweet thing and it is important for you to avoid these sugar crashes right after having a keto meal. We understand there are some organs like the brain of the body that cannot function without glucose, but your body is an amazing machine. It will adapt to the change after some initial issues.

Since Keto diet came into existence due to its numerous, neuroprotective benefits, rest assured, you brain will get the right amount of glucose that is required for its proper functioning.

Flu-Like Symptoms

Like any other thing, your body also resists change. Once you start the Vegan-Keto diet you might develop flu-like symptoms for the first few weeks. You can think of this as your body resisting the need to rely on fats instead of the usual carbs. So, it's important for you to count that amount of fat that is required for your body to functions.

Can cause dizziness and fatigue

Once you completely go on Vegan Ketogenic diet, your insulin levels drop down and fatty acids are released from your body fat. The low insulin level causes the kidneys to start excreting lot of water – you will notice that your trips to the bathroom will increase during this time period- along with potassium and sodium. This can also result in the plummet of your bloody pressure causing fatigue and dizziness.

Might suffer from leg cramps

At the beginning, you will become weak and there are chances that you might suffer from leg cramps because of the fact that your body has run out of electrolytes and fluid. In order to avoid leg cramps it is recommended that you increase the intake of fluid and electrolyte especially during the first few weeks of the diet. You can use vegetable broth as they are really help full.

Reduced Physical Performance

Despite the leg cramps and flu-like symptoms, it is reported that some people even have reduced physical performance during the adaption periods of Keto. For example, if you are an anaerobic, i.e. your sprint or do weight lifting, you might not be able to give your 100 percent due to decreased level of glycogen in your muscles. So, people who are athletes or are their job description requires a lot of physical exertion, should not go on a Vegan Keto diet during the season. They should wait for the time when they are free from their work.

However, the good news is that once your body is over these changes, you will be enjoying the steady, slow-burning energy that results from fat burning instead of quick and fast energy.

SECTION IV:

CHAPTER 8:

RECIPIES

Soy mush

This is recipe is not only filling, but it is also very easy to make. It will only take a few minutes and your kick-start breakfast is ready.

Soy-milk (unsweetened) — 7 oz

Cauliflower — Half

Soy-protein powder — 2 tablespoons

Cinnamon — To taste

Berries of your choice — A small hand full

Directions

Wash the cauliflower and half it. Put it together with the soymilk into a bowl and purée it. Afterwards give the protein powder to it and warm it in a small pot. When finished add the cinnamon and the berries on top.

Protein-power starter

This is your perfect start into the day.

Ingredients

Unsweetened soy yoghurt	1 cup
Coconut milk	¼ cup
Nuts of your choice	1 small hand full
Berries	1/8 cup
Flaxseed oil	1 tablespoon
Chia seeds	2 tablespoons

Direction

Put the yoghurt and the coconut milk together in a bowl. Top with the rest of the ingredients and you have your protein-power starter.

Veggie Chili

An easy and effective vegan recipe that you can enjoy any time of a day!

Kidney beans, Pinto Beans, and Black Beans	one 14.5-oz
Tofu meat	one 14.5-oz
Tomato sauce and Stewed Tomatoes	one 29-oz each
Diced Yellow Onion	Half
Diced Green Bell Pepper with Seeds Removed	Half
Diced Garlic	2-4 cloves
Chili Powder, Black Pepper, and salt	To-taste
Olive oil	3-4 tablespoon

Direction

Start with heating olive oil in a pan on medium high heat. Not put in onions, bell pepper, garlic, and cooks for some time. After that throw in the tofu meat and wait till it gets brown. Now add salt, black pepper and chili powder according to your taste. If you think that taste is still missing you can add more chili powder and salt, also add tomatoes at this stage. Lastly, throw in the tomato sauce, cook for a couple of minutes are you are done.

Chopped Thai Salad with Coconut Curry Dressing

Nothing easier and better than a great salad.

Ingredients

coconut milk	1 can
creamy peanut butter	¼ cup
yellow curry powder	1 tablespoon
clove garlic	1 clove
juice of a lime	to taste
teaspoons sriracha	1-2 teaspoons
salt	1 teaspoon (or to taste)
chopped kale	3 cups
chopped napa cabbage	2 cups
red bell pepper, chopped	1
shredded carrots	1 cup
chopped mango	1 cup

cup chopped peanuts   ½ cup

chopped cilantro   ½ cup

Direction:

Place all ingredients in a blender (coconut milk through salt) and blend on high speed until very smooth. Place dressing in a saucepan, bring to a boil then simmer until reduced and thickened, about 10 minutes. Set aside to cool. Place remaining ingredients into a large bowl, toss with dressing and serve immediately.

Scrambled Tofu

Another one of easy and tasty vegan recipe that you can eat for your breakfast, lunch or dinner

Ingredients

Olive oil	2 tablespoons
Sliced fresh mushrooms	3/4 cup
Tomatoes	2
Garlic, minced	2 cloves
Spinach, rinsed	1 bunch
Firm or extra-firm tofu, well pressed and crumbled	1 pound
Soy sauce	1/2 teaspoons
Lemon juice	1 teaspoon
Salt and pepper	to taste

Direction

Start with heating the oil in a frying pan, and then add onions and garlic. Sauté both of these for a couple of minutes or till they get soft. Now drain the Tofu and press till it becomes fairly dry. Break Tofu and add it in the pan having onions and garlic. Cook on medium heat, and then add in all the vegetables along with the seasoning and cook it for another couple of minutes. Now you are good to go.

The Protein Vegan Salad

Ingredients

Green salad of your choice	2 big hands full
Tofu	3 oz
Red Wine Vinegar	2 tablespoons
Onion	1 chopped
Garlic	1 clove
Dried tomatoes	1oz, chopped to small pieces
Cherry tomatoes	some, according to preference
Vegetable broth	½ cup
Basil	to taste
Olive oil	
Balsamic	

Direction

Roast the onions and the tofu in olive oil. As soon as they get brown, put the garlic and the dried tomatoes with it. Afterwards put a little bit of salt and pepper to it and deglaze with the vegetable broth. Steam it for 10 minutes and after that put 2-3 tablespoons of balsamic to it. Let it cool down.

Afterwards, put the cherry tomatoes, salad, some olive oil and basil with it together into a salad bowl and you are good to go.

Asian Fusion Salad

Ingredients

Red Leaf Lettuce	1 head
Snow Peas	1 cup
Salad Dressing of your choice (Vegan /Lemon Tahini etc.)	¼ tablespoon
Thai Chili Paste	¼ tablespoon
Sesame Oil	1 teaspoon
Soy Sauce	1 teaspoon
Balsamic Vinegar	1 tablespoon
Baked Tofu (Flavored, any)	8-oz
Bean Sprouts	1 ½ cup
Sweet Red Bell	1

Direction

First, wash the lettuce and then cut it into bite sized pieces and after draining put in it a big salad bowl. Cut the tips of snow peas and then cut them into 1-inch slices, also slice cucumber, make sure no slice is longer than 2 inches. After that cut, the red pepper in half, remove the seeds and then make small slices. Wash and drain the bean sprouts. The carrots that you have cut in Julienne style should be boiled for 3 to 4 minutes. After that put in wash them with cold water and drain them. Now add carrots, bean sprouts, red pepper, cucumber and snow peas into the salad bowl. Now cut the tofu into small slices. After that add together chili paste, sesame oil, soy sauce and vinegar and put this mixture over tofu. Put tofu in the center of the salad and you can serve it with any salad dressing of your choice.

Green Salad

Ingredients

Sliced Almonds	½ cup
Mixed Salad Greens	4 cups
Peeled, Cubed Avocado	1
Chopped Garlic	2 Cloves
Fresh Lemon Juice	1 teaspoon
Fresh Parsley (Chopped)	1 teaspoon
White Sugar	1 pinch
Ground Black Pepper	½ teaspoon
Salt	½ teaspoon
Dijon Mustard	1 tablespoon
Olive Oil	4 tablespoons
White Vinegar	2 tablespoons

Direction

This is an amazingly easy to make and yummy to eat salad. Take a large bowl and whisk it with olive oil along with garlic, lemon juice, parsley, sugar, pepper, salt, and mustard. Now add Avocado and stir so that it is coated with all the dressing that you have already placed in the bowl. Just when you are about to serve, add in the salad beans and toss the salad so that everything is mixed well. Now sprinkle sliced almonds on top of it. Your salad is good to go!

SECTION V

CHAPTER 9:

CONCLUSION

Despite its numerous benefits, Vegan Keto diet is something that cannot be recommended for everyone. Below are the people who should not follow this diet plan without doctor's recommendation.

- *Type 1 diabetics*
- *People who are facing metabolic disorder*
- *Women who are planning to get pregnant*
- *Children as they still need carbs for development and growth.*

The rest can enjoy the numerous benefits of this amazing diet plan. Researches and studies have shown that Vegan Keto diet plan not only helps you lose weight, but it also helps reduce some other risk factors including

- *Amyotrophic lateral sclerosis*
- *Acne*
- *Neurological diseases such as Alzheimer's and Parkinson's*
- *Polycystic ovary syndrome*
- *Cancer progression*
- *Type 2 diabetes*
- *Cardiovascular disease*

These are some of the benefits offered by Vegan Keto diet, there are much more. Nonetheless, it is imperative that you have an indebt knowledge regarding your medical situation before you start the diet plan. Once, started it would take you time to adapt it, but after a while, you would start enjoying it.

You can do this for a week, two weeks or even a month, it solely depends upon and your need for the change. Even if you want to permanently adopt this lifestyle, there is no harm. But it all depends upon your will power.

If you liked this book and if it helped you further, please leave a review on Amazon.

Thank you very much for reading!

Yours sincerely

Patrick Price

Made in the USA
San Bernardino, CA
20 August 2017